Ailments of the Hearts and Their Cures

Ibn Taymiyyah

ISBN: 0993669719
ISBN-13: 978-0-9936697-1-2

www.alreshah.com

DEDICATION

To My Mother for Teaching me & To My Grand Parents soul

CONTENTS

ACKNOWLEDGMENTS

Thanks to everyone helped me in this project

CONCERNING THE AILMENTS OF THE HEARTS AND THEIR CURES

Indeed all praise is due to Allah, we seek His help, and we seek His forgiveness, and we seek refuge in Allah from the evil of our souls and the evil of our actions. Whomsoever Allah guides, none can misguide, and whomsoever Allah misguides, none can guide. I bear witness that there is no god worthy of worship except for Allah, the One Who has no partner, and I bear witness that Muhammad is His servant and Messenger. Allah the Exalted said about the hypocrites,

"في قلوبهم مرض فزادهم الله مرضا"   البقرة 11

In their hearts is a disease (of doubt and hypocrisy) and Allâh has increased their disease.   Al-Baqarah 2:11

يجعل ما يلقى الشيطان فتنة للذين في قلوبهم مرض والقاسية قلوبهم وان الظالمين "
"لفي شقاق بعيد   الحج 53

That He (Allâh) may make what is thrown in by Shaitân (Satan) a trial for those in whose hearts is a disease (of hypocrisy and disbelief) and whose hearts are hardened. And certainly, the Zalimûn (polytheists and wrong-doers) are in an opposition far-off (from the truth against Allâh's Messenger and the believers).   Al-Hajj 22:53

لئن لم ينته المنافقون والذين في قلوبهم مرض والمرجفون في المدينة لنغرينك بهم ثم
الأحزاب 60   لا يجاورونك فيها إلا قليلا

If the hypocrites, and those in whose hearts is a disease (evil desire for forbidden sexual relations), and those who spread false news among the people in Al-Madinah stop not, We shall certainly let you overpower them: then they will not be able to stay in it as your neighbours but a little while. Al-Ahzab 33:60

ولا يرتاب الذين أوتوا الكتاب والمؤمنون وليقول الذين في قلوبهم مرض والكافرون
سورة المدثر 31   ماذا اراد الله بهذا مثل

and that no doubt may be left for the people of the Scripture and the believers, and that those in whose hearts is a disease (of hypocrisy) and the disbelievers may say: "What Allâh intends by this (curious) example. Al-Muddathir 74:31

يأيها الناس قد جاءتكم موعظة من ربكم وشفاء لما في الصدور وهدى ورحمة
يونس 57   للمؤمنين

O mankind! There has come to you a good advice from your Lord (i.e. the Qur'ân, enjoining all that is good and forbidding all that is evil), and a healing for that (disease of ignorance, doubt, hypocrisy and differences) which is in your breasts, - a guidance and a mercy (explaining lawful and unlawful things) for the believers. Yunus 10:57

وننزل من القران ما هو شفاء ورحمة للمؤمنين ولا يزيد الظالمين إلا خسارا
الإسراء 82

And We send down of the Qur'ân that which is a healing and a mercy to those who believe (in Islâmic Monotheism and act on it), and it increases the Zâlimûn (polytheists and wrong-doers) nothing but loss. Al-Isra 17:82

ويشف صدور قوم مؤمنين* ويذهب غيظ قلوبهم ويتوب الله على من يشاء والله
التوبة 14-15   عليم حكيم

heal the breasts of Believers, (14) And still the indignation of their hearts. For Allah will turn (in mercy) to whom He will; and Allah is All-Knowing, All-Wise. (15) . At-Tawba 9:14-15

The disease of the body is the opposite of its being sound, and in good health, it is a degeneration that occurs in it causing a failure of the natural senses of perception and movement. So concerning its perception either it goes completely such as blindness or deafness, or it perceives objects incorrectly - such as its perceiving something sweet to be bitter or its hallucinating things that have no reality in the real world. Concerning the failure of its movements then examples of this would be the inability to digest food, or the body's aversion to nourishment that it is need of, or its desire of things that would weaken it, leading to illnesses as a result of these but not leading to death or physical ruin. Instead, these failures would lead to the suffering of the actual body either as a result of consuming a wrong quantity of something or applying something to the body in the wrong way. As for the first, then it could be consuming too little a quantity of nourishment, and therefore the body would require more, or it could be by consuming too much, and therefore the body would require it to be removed. As for the second, then it could be like extremely high or low temperatures due to the incorrect usage of medicine.

The same is true for the disease of the heart for it is a type of degeneration that occurs in it, causing failure in its perception and desires. So concerning its perception then this is degenerated by its being presented with doubts upon doubts until it cannot see the truth or it perceives the truth incorrectly. Its desires are degenerated by its hating the truth which Would be of benefit to it, and loving the falsehood that would cause it harm. So this is why 'diseases' has sometimes been explained to be doubt and suspicion, as was explained by Mujahid and Qatadah in their commentaries to the verse,

البقرة 10   في قلوبهم مرض فزادهم الله مرضا

In their hearts is a disease and Allâh has increased their disease.

Al-Baqarah 2:10

and at other times to be the desire to commit fornication as in the case of the verse,

فيطمع الذي في قلبه مرض وقلن قولا معروفا   سورة الأحزاب 32

Lest one in whose heart is a disease should be moved with desire: but speak ye a speech (that is) just. Al-Ahzab 33:32

The sick person is harmed by things that the healthy person is not, so slight heat, cold, exertion or other such things will harm him due to his inability to endure them in his weakened state. Sickness, in general, weakens the one afflicted by making his endurance weak and unable to sustain what he would have been able to sustain in a strong state. So a healthy state is preserved by remaining healthy and is removed by the opposite, and the sickness is made more severe by the presence of conditions similar to those that led to the sickness in the first place and removed by the opposite. Therefore, if a sick person is afflicted by something similar to that which led him to being sick in the first place, then he increases in illness, and his endurance becomes weaker until maybe he dies. But if he is affected by something that will increase his strength and weaken the illness then the opposite will occur. The disease of the heart is a pain that occurs in the heart such as the anger felt towards an opponent who overcomes you, for this hurts the heart. Allah, the Exalted said,

يشف صدور قوم مؤمنين* ويذهب غيظ قلوبهم ويتوب الله على من شاء والله عليم
حكيم   سورة التوبة 14: 15

Heal the breasts of Believers, (14) And still the indignation of their hearts. For Allah will turn (in mercy) to whom He will; and Allah is All-Knowing, All-Wise. (15) . At-Tawba 9:14-15

So the healing for them was by removing the suffering that had occurred in their hearts, and it is said: 'So and so has healed his anger.' In the case of retaliation, it is said: 'The close relatives of the killed sought to heal,' meaning healing of their grief, anger, and sorrow - all of these being sufferings that occur in oneself Likewise doubt and ignorance cause pain to the heart. The Prophet (ﷺ) said, "Could they not have asked if they did not know? Indeed the cure for ignorance is to ask." And the one who doubts something he has taken on board causes harm to his heart until he attains knowledge and certainty. Hence it is said to a scholar when he answers in a way that clarifies the truth: 'you have healed me with the answer.'

BETWEEN SICKNESS AND DEATH

Sickness is of a lesser level than death, so the heart dies due to total ignorance but becomes ill due to having fragments of ignorance, and in this case, there can be either death, sickness or healing for the heart. Its life, death, sickness and the cure is greater and more vital than the life, death, sickness, and cure of the body. This is why the heart becomes sick when presented with doubts and desires, or the sickness becomes acuter. If wisdom and goodly exhortation occur then theses are routes to its correction and cure. Allah, the Highest, says,

ليجعل الله ما يلقي الشيطان فتنة للذين في قلوبهم مرض والقاسية قلوبهم وإن الظالمين لفي شقاق بعيد   الحج 53

That He (Allâh) may make what is thrown in by Shaitân (Satan) a trial for those in whose hearts is a disease (of hypocrisy and disbelief) and whose hearts are hardened. And certainly, the Zalimûn (polytheists and wrong-doers) are in an opposition far-off (from the truth against Allâh's Messenger and the believers). Al-Hajj 22:53

Because this breeds doubts in them and their hearts harden due to their dryness, and are weakened by doubt and become distant from faith and therefore what is thrown in by Satan becomes a trial for them. Allah, the Highest, said,

لئن لم ينته المنافقون والذين في قلوبهم مرض والمرجفون في المدينة لنغرينك بهم ثم لا يجاورونك إلا قليلا   الأحزاب 60

If the hypocrites and those in whose hearts is disease and those who spread rumors in al-Madinah do not cease, We will surely incite you against them; then they will not remain your neighbors therein except for a little.

وَلاَ يَرْتَابَ الَّذِينَ أُوتُوا الْكِتَابَ وَالْمُؤْمِنُونَ وَلِيَقُولَ الَّذِينَ فِي قُلُوبِهِم مَّرَضٌ وَالْكَافِرُونَ
المدثر 31 مَاذَا أَرَادَ اللَّـهُ بِهَـذَا مَثَلاً

and that no doubt may be left for the people of the Scripture and the believers, and that those in whose hearts is a disease (of hypocrisy) and the disbelievers may say: "What Allâh intends by this (curious) example ?" These people's heart (which have hardened) have not died as in the case of the disbelievers and the hypocrites, and neither are their hearts correct and pure like the pure hearts of the believers, rather they contain the sickness of doubt and desire. The same applies to (the ones referred to in) His saying:

سورة الأحزاب 32 فيطمع الذي في قلبه مرض وقلن قولا معروفا

lest one in whose heart is a disease should be moved with desire: but speak ye a speech (that is) just. Al-Ahzab 33:32

Referring to the sickness of desire, for indeed if the correct heart is tempted by a woman it will not incline towards her, contrary to the heart diseased with desire, for it, due to its weakness, will incline towards what it is tempted with in accordance with the strength or the weakness of the sickness, and when it submits to the temptation, the sickness in the heart is satiated.

THE QUR'AN IS A CURE FOR THE HEARTS

The Qur'an is a cure for that which is within the heart, and for the one who has the sickness of doubt and desire in his heart, for it contains clear proofs that distinguish the truth from falsehood, and remove the sickness of false doubts to leave certain knowledge, correct perception and understanding such that the heart sees things in accordance to their reality It contains wisdom, goodly exhortations both encouraging good and deterring from evil, and stories which contain lessons that necessarily lead to the correction of the heart by making the heart desire what is good for it and detest what is harmful to it. Hence the heart is left desiring that which will guide it, hating that which will deviate it after it used to desire that which would deviate it and hate that which would guide it. The Qur'an removes all the sicknesses that invoke false desires until the heart becomes pure and therefore its desires become pure and it returns to the natural state (fitrah) that it was created in, just as the body returns to the natural state upon being treated. The heart will be nurtured with faith and the Qur'an such that it will become strong - for indeed the purification of the heart is like the growing   of   the   body.

RIGHTEOUS ACTIONS ARE A CURE FOR THE HEART

Zakah (purification) in the language means growth and increase in correction, it is said, 'something has Zakah\ when it has grown in correction. The heart is in need of being nurtured so that it may mature and increase until it becomes complete and correct just as the body is in need of nourishment that is good for it, but along with this, there is a need to prevent anything from harming it. So the body will not grow until it gains that which will benefit it and is prevented from that which will harm it, likewise the heart will not become pure such that it may grow and become complete with respect to its correction, until it attains that which benefits it and represses that which harms it - just as the flower will not grow without these two factors. Sadaqah (charity), due to its extinguishing the sins as water extinguishes the fire, causes the heart to be purified. Its zakah means something additional to it being merely free of sins. Allah the Exalted said,

خذ من أموالهم صدقة تطهرهم وتزكيهم بها وصل عليهم   التوبة 103

Take Sadaqah (alms) from their wealth in order to purify them and sanctify them with it. At-Tawbah 9:103

Leaving Indecent Actions are a Cure for the Heart

Similarly abstaining from indecent actions and sins leads to purification of the heart, for these are of the same level as leprosy of the body or thorns on a flower. So when the body is freed of this leprosy by releasing the additional blood, for example, the natural strength of the body emerges and it can find relief and thereby grow. Likewise when one seeks repentance from sin, the heart is released from contamination - whereby it mixed the righteous actions with evils actions, so when one repents from sins the strength of the heart emerges as does its desire to perform righteous actions and it finds relief from these false and corrupt matters that it was submerged in. So the zakah of the heart means its growing and becoming complete. Allah the Exalted said,

ولولا فضل الله عليكم ورحمته ما زكى منكم من أحد أبا ولكن الله يزكي   النور 21

And had it not been for the Grace of Allâh and His Mercy on you, not one of you would ever have been pure from sins. AN-Nur 24:21

فأن لم تجدوا فيها أحدا فلا تدخلوها حتى يؤذن لكم وإن قيل لكم ارجعوا هو أزكى لكم والله بما تعلمون عليم   النور 28

And if you are asked to go back, go back, for it is purer for you. And Allâh is All-Knower of what you do. AN-Nur 24:28

قل للمؤمنين يغضوا من أبصارهم ويحفظوا من فروجهم ذلك أزكى لهم عن الله خبير بما يصنعون   النور 30

Tell the believing men to lower their gaze (from looking at forbidden things), and protect their private parts (from illegal sexual acts). That is purer for them. An-Nur 24:30

قد أفلح من تزكى* وذكر اسم ربه فصلى   الأعلى 14-15

Indeed whosoever purifies himself (by avoiding polytheism and accepting Islâmic Monotheism) shall achieve success,15. And remembers (glorifies) the Name of his Lord (worships none but Allâh), and prays (five compulsory prayers and Nawâfil - additional prayers).   Al-A'la 87:15-14

قد أفلح من زكاها* وقد خاب من دساها   الشمس 9-10

Indeed he succeeds who purifies his ownself (i.e. obeys and performs all that Allâh ordered, by following the true Faith of Islamic Monotheism and by doing righteous good deeds).10. And indeed he fails who corrupts his own self (i.e. disobeys what Allâh has ordered by rejecting the true Faith of Islâmic Monotheism or by following polytheism or by doing every kind of evil wicked deeds). Ash-Shamas 91:10-9

وما يدريك لعله يزكى   عبس 3

And how can you know that he might become pure (from sins)?. Abasa 80:3

فقل هل لك إلى ان تزكى* أهديك إلى ربك فتخشى"   النازعات 18-19

And say to him: "Would you purify yourself (from the sin of disbelief by becoming a believer)?" 19. "And that I guide you to your Lord, so you should fear Him?" An-Nazi'at 79:19-18

So tazkiyyah (purification), even if its basic meaning is growth, blessing, and increase in goodness, is only attained by removing the evil, and this is why purification has come to combine both these matters (i.e., performing good and avoiding evil). He, the Highest, said,

وويل للمشركين * الذين لا يؤتون الزكاة وهم بالأخرة هم كافرون   فصلت 6-7

and seek forgiveness of Him. And woe to Al-Mushrikûn (the polytheists, idolaters, disbelievers in the Oneness of Allâh).7. Those who give not the Zakât and they are disbelievers in the Hereafter. Fussilat 41:7-6

Meaning by zikah, the Tawhid and iman by which the heart is purified, for indeed tawhid includes negating any lordship besides Allah and affirming the Lordship of Allah in the heart, this being the reality of 'La Ilaha Ila Allah' (there is none worthy of worship except Allah) and this being the basis by which the hearts are purified. Meaning by zikah, the Tawhid and iman by which the heart is purified, for indeed tawhid includes negating any lordship besides Allah and affirming the Lordship of Allah in the heart, this being the reality of 'La Ilaha Ilia Allah' (there is none worthy of worship except Allah) and this being the basis by which the hearts are purified.

فلا تزكوا أنفسكم   النجم 32

So ascribe not purity to yourselves. do not broadcast that you are pure, and this is not the same as His saying. An-Najm 53:32

قد أفلح من تزكى   الشمس 9

Indeed he succeeds who purifies his ownself (i.e. obeys and performs all that Allâh ordered, by following the true Faith of Islâmic Monotheism and by doing righteous good deeds). This is why Allah, the Most High, said,

هو أعلم بمن اتقى   سورة النجم 32

He knows best him who fears Allâh and keeps his duty to Him Zaynab was initially known as Burra, and it is said that she purified herself and so the Messenger of Allah (ﷺ) called her Zaynab. As for the saying of Allah,

ألم تر إلى الذين يزكون أنفسهم بل الله يزكي من يشاء   النساء 49

Have you not seen those (Jews and Christians) who claim sanctity for themselves. Nay, but Allâh sanctifies whom He wills, An-Nisa 4:49

Meaning He makes pure whomsoever He pleases and makes his purity known, just as the purifier declares to be pure only those whose justice he can bear testimony to.

The Effect of Sins Upon the Purity of the Heart

Adl (fairness and justice) is I'tidal (balance), and in balance lies the correction of the heart, just as in zulm (imbalance/ oppression) lies its corruption. This is why for every sin that the person has committed he has oppressed his self (zaliman li nafsihi). The opposite of zulm is, so this sinful person has not been just to his self rather he has oppressed it. The correction of the heart lies in (adl, and its corruption lies in zulm. Therefore, when the servant oppresses himself, he is the oppressor and oppressed at the same time, likewise when he is just then he is the one who is just and the one upon whom the justice is carried out. The person does an action, and he will receive the fruit of this action, be it bitter or sweet. Allah said,

البقرة 286   لها ما كسبت وعليها ما اكتسبت

He gets a reward for that (good) which he has earned, and he is punished for that (evil) which he has earned. Al-Baqarah 2:286

Aml (actions) have an effect upon the heart, either of benefit, harm, or correction before they effect the external body. The good and pure actions constitute justice for the soul whereas bad actions oppress the soul. Allah the Most High, said,

فصلت 41   من عمل صالحا فلنفسه ومن أساء فعليها وماربك بظلام للعبيد

Whosoever does righteous good deed, it is for (the benefit of) his ownself; and whosoever does evil, it is against his ownself. And your Lord is not at all unjust to (His) slaves. Fussilat 41:41

سورة الإسراء7   إن أحسنتم أحسنتم لأنفسكم وإن أسأتم فلها

"If you do good, you do good for your own selves, and if you do evil (you do it) against yourselves." Al-Isra 17:7

Some of the Salaf said, 'Indeed good actions are a light in the heart, a strengthening For the body, a glow on the face, a cause for extensive provisions and love in the hearts of the creation. Indeed bad actions are darkness in the heart, a blackness on the face, a weakness for the body, a cause for decrease in provisions and hatred in the hearts of the creation.' Allah, the Most High, said,

سورة الطور21   كل امرئ بما كسب رهين

Every person, for what he earned, is retained. At-Tur 52:21

 And those who believe and whose offspring follow them in Faith: to them shall We join their offspring, and We shall not decrease the reward of their deeds in anything. Every person is a pledge for that which he has earned.

كل نفس بما كسبت رهينة   المدثر 38

Every soul will be (held) in pledge for its deeds. (38) Except the Companions of the Right Hand. (39) Al-Muddathir 74:38-39

(i.e. the pious true believers of Islamic Monotheism)

وذكر به ان تبسل نفس بما كسبت ليس لها من دون الله ولي ولا شفيع وإن تعدل كل عدل لا يؤخذ منها أولئك الذين أبسلوا بما كسبوا   الانعام 70

And leave alone those who take their religion as play and amusement, and whom the life of this world has deceived. But remind (them) with it (the Qur'an) lest a person be given up to destruction for that which he has earned, when he will find for himself no protector or intercessor besides Allah, and even if he offers every ransom, it will not be accepted from him. Such are they who are given up to destruction because of that which they have earned Tubsala means: to-repress, to fetter and captivate. Similarly, when the body has recovered from illness it is said: 'He has balanced his temperament and disposition.' This is because the sickness distorts the temperament, despite the fact that there is no way to achieve complete balance, safe from mixing both justice and injustice - but the ideal or close to the ideal should be aimed for.

The same case applies to the heart, its health and correction lies in the balance, and its sickness lies in deviation, oppression, and digression. But complete balance in everything is impossible, in action or knowledge - but the ideal or the closest to the ideal should be aimed for. This is why it is said, describing the Salaji way: 'the ideal way.' Allah said

ولن تستطيعوا أن تعدلوا بين النساء ولو حرصتم فلا تميلوا كل الميل   النساء
129

You will never be able to do perfect justice between wives even if it is your ardent desire. An-Nisa 4:129

وأوفوا الكيل والميزان بالقسط لا نكلف نفسا إلا وسعها   الأنعام 152

And give full measure and full weight with justice. We burden not any person, but that which he can bear. Al-An'am 6:152

Allah, the Exalted, sent the messengers and revealed the Books so that man may establish justice, and the greatest form of justice is to worship Allah alone with no partner; then giving due justice to the rights of man; then being just upon oneself.

Types of Zulm

Zulm is of three types, and all of these are from the sicknesses of the heart, and in justice lies its good health and purity. Imam Ahmad bin Hanbal said to one of the people, 'If you were healthy you would not fear anyone,' meaning that the fear you have of men is due to sickness from within you, such as the sickness of shirk and sins. The basis of the heart being corrected lies in it being alive and enlightened. Allah, the Most High, said,

أومن كان ميتا فأحييناه وجعلنا له نورا يمشي به في الناس كمن هو في الظلمات ليس بخارج منها   الأنعام 122

Is he who was dead (without Faith by ignorance and disbelief) and We gave him life (by knowledge and Faith) and set for him a light (of Belief) whereby he can walk amongst men - like him who is in the darkness (of disbelief, polytheism, and hypocrisy) from which he can never come out?

This is why Allah has mentioned the life of the heart, its illumination, death, and darkness in a number of places, like His, the Exalted's saying,

لينذر من كان حيا   يس 70

That he or it (Muhammad صلى الله عليه وسلم or the Qur'ân) may give warning to him who is living (a healthy minded - the believer). Ya seen 36:70

يا أيها الذين ءامنوا استجيبوا لله وللرسول اذا دعاكم لما يحييكم واعلموا أن الله يحول بين المرء وقلبه وأنه إليه تحشرون
الأنفال 24

O you who believe! Answer Allâh (by obeying Him) and (His) Messenger when he (صلى الله عليه وسلم) calls you to that which will give you life, and know that Allâh comes in between a person and his heart (i.e., He prevents an evil person to decide anything). And verily to Him, you shall (all) be gathered. Al-Anfal 8:24

يخرج الحي من الميت ويخرج الميت من الحي   الروم19

He brings out the living from the dead and brings out the dead from the living. And He revives the earth after its death. Ar-Rum 30:19

From the examples of this is His bringing forth a believer from a disbeliever, and a disbeliever from a believer. In the authentic hadith, The similitude of a house in which Allah is mentioned, and the house in which Allah is not mentioned is as the living and the dead. In the Sahib (of al-Bukhari) is the hadith, Perform some of your prayers in your houses, and do not take them as graves. Allah, the Most High, has said,

والذين كذبوا بآياتنا صم وبكم في الظلمات   الأنعام 39

Those who reject Our Ayat (proofs, evidence, verses, lessons, signs, revelations, etc.) are deaf and dumb in the darkness. Al-An'am 6:39

Allah has mentioned the 'Verse of Light' and the 'Verse of Darkness' saying,

الله نور السموات والأرض مثل نوره كمشكاة فيها مصباح المصباح في زجاجه الزجاجة كأنها كوكب دري يوقد من شجرة مباركة زيتونة لا شرقية ولا غربية يكاد زيتها يضيئ ولو لم تمسسه نار نور على نور يهدي الله لنوره   النور 35

Allah is the Light of the heavens and the earth. The parable of His Light is as (if there were) a niche and within it a lamp: the lamp is in a glass, the glass as it were a brilliant star, lit from a blessed tree, an olive, neither of the east (i.e. neither it gets sun-rays only in the morning) nor of the west (i.e. nor it gets sun-rays only in the afternoon, but it is exposed to the sun all day long), whose oil would almost glow forth (of itself), though no fire touched it. Light upon Light! This is the similitude for the light of faith in the hearts of the believers. An-Nur 24:35 Then He said,

والذين كفروا أعمالهم كسراب بقيعة يحسبه الظمئان ماء حتى إذا جاءه لم يجده شيئا
ووجد الله عنده فوفاه حسابه والله سريع الحساب أو كظلمات في بحر لجي يغشاه موج
من فوقه موج من فوقه سحاب ظلمات بعضها فوق بعض إذا اخرج يده لم يكد يراها
ومن لم يجعل الله له نورا فما له من نور   النور 39 - 40

As for those who disbelieve, their deeds are like a mirage in a desert. The thirsty one thinks it to be water, until he comes up to it, he finds it to be nothing; but he finds Allâh with him, Who will pay him his due (Hell). And Allâh is Swift in taking account. 39. Or [the state of a disbeliever] is like the darkness in a vast deep sea, overwhelmed with waves topped by waves, topped by dark clouds, (layers of) darkness upon darkness: if a man stretches out his hand, he can hardly see it! And he for whom Allâh has not appointed light, for him there is no light. An-Nur 24:40-39

So the first verse (no. 39) sets forth a similitude for the false beliefs and the actions that arise from these beliefs, one considers them to be something of benefit, but when they come to him (on the day of Judgement), he will not find any benefit in them at all. Rather Allah will fully give him his recompense for these actions (in Hell). The second verse (no. 40) is the similitude propounded for extensive ignorance, lack of faith and (correct) knowledge. The person who possesses these is in darknesses one above another, unable to see anything, for indeed the sight occurs only with the light of faith and (correct) knowledge. Allah, the Most High, said,

إن الذين اتقوا إذا مسهم طائف من الشيطان تذكروا فإذا هم مبصرون
الأعراف 7

Verily, those who are Al-Muttaqûn, when an evil thought comes to them from Shaitân (Satan), they remember (Allâh), and (indeed) they then see (aright). Al-A'raf 7:7

ولقد همت به وهم بها لولا أن رءا برهان ربه   يوسف 24

And indeed she did desire him, and he would have inclined to her desire, had he not seen the evidence of his Lord. Yusuf 12:24

Meaning the proof of faith which his heart had attained, so due to this Allah caused him to turn away from that which he was inclined to, and recorded for him a complete good deed, and no sin was recorded against him due to his having performed a good action and not performed an evil one. Allah, the Exalted said,

الٓر كتاب أنزلناه إليك لتخرج الناس من الظلمات إلى النور بإذن ربهم إلى صراط العزيز الحميد   ابراهيم 1

Alif-Lâm-Râ. [These letters are one of the miracles of the Qur'an, and none but Allah (Alone) knows their meanings]. (This is) A Book which We have revealed unto you (O Muhammad صلى الله عليه و سلم) in order that you might lead mankind out of darkness (of disbelief and polytheism) into light (of belief in the Oneness of Allah and Islamic Monotheism) by their Lord's Leave to the Path of the All-Mighty, the Owner of all Praise. Ibrahim 14:1

الله ولي الذين ءامنوا يخرجهم من الظلمات إلى النور والذين كفروا أولياؤهم الطاغوت يخرجونهم من النور إلى الظلمات   البقرة 257

Allah is the Walî (Protector or Guardian) of those who believe. He brings them out from darkness into light. But as for those who disbelieve, their Auliyâ (supporters and helpers) are Tâghût [false deities and false leaders], they bring them out from light into darkness. Al-Baqara 2:257

يا أيها الذين ءامنوا اتقوا الله و ءامنوا برسوله يؤتكم كفلين من رحمته ويجعل لكم نورا تمشون به ويغفر لكم والله غفور رحيم   الحديد 28

O you who believe [in Mûsâ (Moses) (i.e., Jews) and 'Îsâ (Jesus) (i.e., Christians)]! Fear Allâh, and believe in His Messenger (Muhammad ﷺ), He will give you a double portion of His Mercy, and He will give you a light by which you shall walk (straight). And He will forgive you. And Allâh is Oft-Forgiving, Most Merciful. Al-Hadid 57:28

This is why Allah has propounded two types of parables for faith: a parable of water by which life exists and the foam which comes with it; and a parable of the tire by which light is produced. Allah said,

أنزل من السماء ماء فسالت اودية بقدرها فاحتمل السيل زبدا رابيا ومما يوقدون عليه في النار ابتغاء حلية أو متاع زبد مثله كذلك يضرب الله الحق والباطل فأما الزبد فيذهب جفاء   الرعد   17

He sends down water (rain) from the sky, and the valleys flow according to their measure, but the flood bears away the foam that mounts up to the surface - and (also) from that (ore) which they heat in the fire in order to make ornaments or utensils, rises a foam like unto it, thus does Allâh (by parables) show forth truth and falsehood. Similarly, Allah has propounded two parables for hypocrisy. Ar-Ra'd 13:17

مثلهم كمثل الذي استوقد نارا فلما أضاءت ما حوله ذهب الله بنورهم وتركهم في ظلمات لا يبصرون* صم بكم عمي فهم لا يرجعون* أو كصيب من السماء فيه ظلمات ورعد وبرق يجعلون أصابعهم في آذانهم من الصواعق حذر الموت والله محيط بالكافرين* يكاد البرق يخطف أبصارهم كلما أضاء لهم مشوا فيه وإذا أظلم عليهم قاموا ولو شاء الله لذهب بسمعهم وأبصارهم إن الله على كل شيء قدير
البقرة 17-20

Their likeness is as the likeness of one who kindled a fire; then, when it lighted all around him, Allâh took away their light and left them in darkness. (So) They could not see.17. They are deaf, dumb, and blind, so they return not (to the Right Path).18. Or like a rainstorm from the sky, wherein is darkness, thunder, and lightning. They thrust their fingers in their ears to keep out the stunning thunder-clap for fear of death. But Allâh ever encompasses the disbelievers (i.e., Allâh will gather them all together).19. The lightning almost snatches away their sight, whenever it flashes for them, they walk therein, and when darkness covers them, they stand still. And if Allâh willed, He could have taken away their hearing and their sight. Certainly, Allâh has power over all things. Al-Baqara 2:17-20

So He propounded a parable for them with one who kindled a fire, each time it ignited Allah caused it to extinguish, and the parable of water in which the water is sent down containing darkness, thunder, and lightning - this is not the place for a detailed explanation of these parables for the purpose here is only to mention the life of the heart and its illumination.

THE LIFE OF THE HEART

In the narrated du*a there occurs, Make the Qur'an the nurturer (rabie') of our hearts and the light of our chest.

Rabie': means the rain that descends from the sky and nourishes the plants. The Arabs call the season in which the rain first descends al-Rabie' due to the fall of rain which causes growth (of produce). The non-Arabs call the season that follows winter al-Rabie' because in this season the plants from which fruit is produced blossom and the leaves on the trees appear.

The State of the Dead Heart

The heart that is alive and enlightened hears, sees and understands due to the light that it contains, while the dead heart does not hear, see or understand. Allah, the Exalted said

مثل الذين كفروا كمثل الذي ينعق بما لا يسمع إلا دعاء ونداء صم بكم عمي فهم لا
يعقلون   البقرة 171

And the example of those who disbelieve is as that of him who shouts to those (flock of sheep) that hears nothing but calls and cries. (They are) Deaf, dumb and blind. So they do not understand. Al-Baqara 2:171 (Tafsîr Al-Qurtubi)

ومنهم من يستمعون إليك أفأنت تسمع الصم ولو كانوا لا يعقلون* ومنهم من ينظر
إليك أفأنت تهدي العمي ولو كانوا لا يبصرون
يونس 42-43

And among them are some who listen to you, but can you make the deaf to hear - even though they apprehend not?. 42. And among them are some who look at you, but can you guide the blind - even though they see not?. Yunus 10: 43-42

وَمِنْهُم مَّن يَسْتَمِعُ إِلَيْكَ وَجَعَلْنَا عَلَى قُلُوبِهِمْ أَكِنَّةً أَن يَفْقَهُوهُ وَفِي آذَانِهِمْ وَقْرًا وَإِن يَرَوْا
كُلَّ آيَةٍ لاَّ يُؤْمِنُوا بِهَا حَتَّى إِذَا جَاؤُوكَ يُجَادِلُونَكَ يَقُولُ الَّذِينَ كَفَرُوا إِنْ هَذَآ إِلاَّ أَسَاطِيرُ

21

الأوّلِينَ   الأنعام 25

And of them there are some who listen to you; but We have set veils on their hearts, so they understand it not, and deafness in their ears; and even if they see every one of the Ayât (proofs, evidence, verses, lessons, signs, revelations, etc.) they will not believe therein; to the point that when they come to you to argue with you, the disbelievers say: "These are nothing but tales of the men of old." Al-An'am 6:25

So He informed us that their hearts could not understand, and their ears cannot hear, and they do not believe in what they have seen of the Fire as He informed us about them when He said,

وَقَالُوا قُلُوبُنَا فِي أَكِنَّةٍ مِّمَّا تَدْعُونَا إِلَيْهِ وَفِي آذانِنَا وَقْرٌ وَمِن بَيْنِنَا وَبَيْنِكَ حِجَاب فصلت 5

And they say: "Our hearts are under coverings (screened) from that to which you invite us, and in our ears is deafness, and between us and you is a screen. Fussilat 41:5

So they mentioned the barriers upon their hearts, ears and eves. Their bodies are alive - hearing and seeing, but this is a life of the body devoid of life in the heart - like the life of an animal - for the animals possess hearing and seeing, and eat and drink and marry.

This is why Allah said,

وَمَثَلُ الَّذِينَ كَفَرُوا كَمَثَلِ الَّذِي يَنْعِقُ بِمَا لَا يَسْمَعُ إِلَّا دُعَاء وَنِدَاء صُمٌّ بُكْمٌ عُمْيٌ فَهُمْ لَا يَعْقِلُونَ   البقرة 171

And the example of those who disbelieve is as that of him who shouts to those (flock of sheep) that hears nothing but calls and cries. (They are) Deaf, dumb and blind. So they do not understand. Al-Baqara 2:171 (Tafsîr Al-Qurtubi)

Likening them to the cattle, at whom the shepherd shouts, and they hear nothing except the cry (not understanding what is said), as He said in other verses,

أَمْ تَحْسَبُ أَنّ أَكْثَرَهُمْ يَسْمَعُونَ أَوْ يَعْقِلُونَ إِنْ هُمْ إِلاَّ كَالأَنْعَامِ بَلْ هُمْ أَضَلُّ سَبِيلاً
الفرقان 44

Or do you think that most of them hear or understand? They are only like cattle - nay, they are even farther astray from the Path (i.e. even worse than cattle). Al-Furqan 25:44

وَلَقَدْ ذَرَأْنَا لِجَهَنَّمَ كَثِيرًا مِّنَ الْجِنِّ وَالإِنس لَهُمْ قُلُوبٌ لاَّ يَفْقَهُونَ بِهَا وَلَهُمْ أَعْيُنٌ لاَّ
يُبْصِرُونَ بِهَا وَلَهُمْ آذَانٌ لاَّ يَسْمَعُونَ بِهَا أُوْلَـئِكَ كَالأَنْعَامِ بَلْ هُمْ أَضَلُّ أُوْلَـئِكَ هُمُ الْغَافِلُونَ
الأعراف 179

And surely, We have created many of the jinn and mankind for Hell. They have hearts wherewith they understand not, and they have eyes wherewith they see not, and they have ears wherewith they hear not (the truth). They are like cattle, nay even more astray; those! They are the heedless ones. Al-A'raf 7:179

A group of the commentators, when referring to these verses and those that resembled them such as the verse,

وَإِذَا مَسَّ الإِنسَانَ الضُّرُّ دَعَانَا لِجَنبِهِ أَوْ قَاعِدًا أَوْ قَآئِمًا فَلَمَّا كَشَفْنَا عَنْهُ ضُرَّهُ مَرَّ كَأَن
لَّمْ يَدْعُنَا إِلَى ضُرٍّ مَّسَّهُ   يونس 12

And when harm touches man, he invokes Us, lying on his side, or sitting or standing. But when We have removed his harm from him, he passes on as if he had never invoked Us for a harm that touched him! Yunus 10:12

Regarding these and other such verses that mention the faults of man and their condemnation, (the commentators) said, These verses refer to the disbelievers, and that the meaning of 'man' here is 'the disbelievers.' So the one who hears this explanation is left thinking that one who openly manifests Islam is not included in this condemnation and threat, rather his thoughts link (these verses) to those who openly manifested shirk from amongst the Arabs, or to those he knows to have openly shown disbelief such as the Jews, the Christians and the polytheists of Turkey and India - and hence he would not benefit from these verses that Allah revealed so that His servants may be guided. So it is said in reply that firstly: those that openly manifest Islam include amongst them the believer and hypocrite, and the hypocrites are many in all periods of time, and they are in the lowest level of the He'll fire.

Secondly: man possesses a strain of hypocrisy and disbelief even if he possesses faith along with this, as the Prophet (ﷺ) said in the hadith reported by both al-Bukharl and Muslim, "There are four qualities which if found in a person make him a pure hypocrite, and the one who has a portion of them has a portion of hypocrisy until he leaves them: when he speaks he lies, when he is entrusted, he betrays, when he speaks, he speak a lie, when he makes a covenant, he proves treacherous, when he quarrels, he behaves in an evil and insulting manner . So he informed us that the one who has a portion of these then he has a portion of hypocrisy, and it is established in the Sahib of al-Bukhari that he said to Abu Dhar. Indeed you have displayed a trait of Jahiliyyah in you. And Abu Dhar was from the most truthful of people with respect to his faith. He (ﷺ) said in the authentic ahadith, Four (traits) in my Ummah are from the matters of jdhiliyyah (pre-Islamic ignorance): boasting about noble descent, abusing the lineage, wailing [over the dead] and seeking rain from the stars. You will indeed follow the ways of those that came before you, inch by inch such that if they were to enter a lizard hole, you too would do so. They asked, 'Do you mean the Jews and Christians?' He replied, 'Who else?' What the early nations took to shall also be taken to by my nation, cubit by cubit and handspan by handspan. They said, 'Do you mean the Persians and the Romans.' To which he replied, 'Who else from amongst the people could it be.' Ibn Abi-Mulaykah said I met thirty of the Companions of Muhammad all of them fearing hypocrisy for themselves. And from 'All - or i ludhayfah - that he said, The heart are of four types: the clear heart that is illuminated by a torch - this is the heart of the believer. The encased heart - this is the heart of the disbeliever, the inverted heart - this is the heart of the hypocrite, and the heart that has two attractions, a time when it is called to faith, and a time when it is called to hypocrisy - these are a people that have mixed good actions with evil ones. So when this is understood, it becomes known that every servant benefits from what Allah mentioned concerning faith, either extolling the branches of faith or censuring the branches of disbelief. The case mentioned above is similar to what some of them ask concerning His saying,

اهدنا الصراط المستقيم   الفاتحة 6

Guide us to the Straight Way. Al-Fatiha 1:6

saying: 'Allah has already guided the believer, so what benefit is there in seeking guidance?' Then some of them reply by saying that the meaning is 'keep us firm upon guidance' as the Arab would say to the one who is asleep, 'sleep until I come to you.' Others from amongst them say that the meaning is, 'keep our hearts firm upon the guidance' and that the request for firmness has been omitted. Yet others from amongst them say that it means, 'increase me in guidance.' This question really occurs due to the absence of their contemplating upon the Straight Path to which the servant seeks guidance to, for the meaning [of the verse] is [seeking guidance to] act according to what Allah ordered, and leave what He forbade in all matters.

THE NEED FOR BENEFICIAL KNOWLEDGE

This is because the person, even if he has believed that Muhammad is the Messenger of Allah and that the Qur'an is the truth in a general way, is commonly in need of knowledge of that which would benefit him and harm him. He is in need of knowledge concerning what he has been commanded to do and forbidden from doing in the finer aspects of the matters and in those areas of which he has no knowledge. [Not only this but we find that] that which he does have knowledge of, he does not put the greater part of it to practice! Assuming that all of the commands and prohibitions contained in the Qur'an and Sunnah have reached him, then the Qur'an and Sunnah contain laws that are general and universal for which it is not possible to specify to every individual person - therefore the person has been commanded due to the likes of this to ask for guidance to the Straight Path.

Guidance to the Straight Path includes all of the following matters: cognizance of what the Messenger (ﷺ) came with in detail, cognizance of what comes under his general orders and concern for acting according to ones knowledge, for indeed just having knowledge is not a cause for attaining guidance if one does not act according to his knowledge. This is why He said to His Prophet (ﷺ) after the treaty of hudaybiyy,

إِنَّا فَتَحْنَا لَكَ فَتْحًا مُبِينًا* لِيَغْفِرَ لَكَ اللّهُ مَا تَقَدَّمَ مِن ذَنبِكَ وَمَا تَأَخَّرَ وَيُتِمَّ نِعْمَتَهُ عَلَيْكَ وَيَهْدِيَكَ صِرَاطًا مُسْتَقِيمًا   1- 2 الفتح

Verily, We have given you (O Muhammad صلى الله عليه وسلم) a manifest victory.2. That Allâh may forgive you your sins of the past and the future,.1. and complete His Favour on you, and guide you on the Straight Path, Al-Fath 48:1-2

And He said with respect to Musa and Harun,

وَآتَيْنَاهُمَا الْكِتَابَ الْمُسْتَبِينَ * وَهَدَيْنَاهُمَا الصِّرَاطَ الْمُسْتَقِيمَ

And We gave them the clear Scripture;117. And guided them to the Right Path. As-Saffat 37:117-118

The Muslims have differed as to what Allah Willed from the textual matters - matters of knowledge, belief and action while all of them are agreed that Muhammad is the truth and the Quran is the truth. If all of them were to have attained guidance to the Straight Path in totality, then they would never have differed. Furthermore, the majority of those who know what Allah has ordered disobey Him and do not follow His Way. If they were guided to the Straight Path in these matters, then they certainly would have performed what they had been commanded to do, and left what they had been forbidden from. As for those whom Allah guided from amongst this nation until they became from the God-Fearing Friends of Allah, then the greatest reason for this was their supplicating to Allah with this supplication,

اهدنا الصراط المستقيم   الفاتحة 6

Guide us to the Straight Way. Al-Fatiha 1:6.

In every prayer along with the knowledge of their continuous need of Allah that He guide them on the Straight Path, So due to their continually saying this supplication and their acknowledging their continuous need of Him they became God-Fearing Friends of Allah. Sahl bin 'Abdullah at-Tustori said, There is not route between a servant and Allah closer to Him then need. The one who has attained guidance in the past is in need of guidance in the future, this is the real meaning behind the saying of those who say that it means: 'establish us and guide us to being firm upon the Straight Path.' The opinion of those who say that it means: 'increase us in guidance' includes what has preceded. But all that has been stated refers to His guidance to the Straight Path that is to be granted in the future, for indeed action in the future is upon the knowledge that is not yet attained. And the person is not

27

considered to be one who is guided until he acts according to his knowledge in the future, but it is possible that this knowledge not be there in the future, rather it could be removed from the heart, and if it still be there it is also possible that it not be acted upon. Therefore all of mankind is in dire need of this supplication; this is why Allah made it obligatory upon them in every prayer, and they are not in need of any other supplication as they are of this one. When guidance is obtained to the Straight Path then help, provision and all of the happiness that the soul seeks are obtained [from Allah]. Allah knows best.

The Reality of the Life of the Heart

Know that the life of the heart and other than it is not merely one of sensation, movement, and intent, or merely one of knowledge and ability as assumed and intent, or merely one of knowledge and ability as assumed by a group of investigators into the Knowledge of Allah and His power such as Abu al-Husain aL-Basrl. They said; He can only be considered to have Life as long as He Knows and is Able.

This is not the case, rather life is an attribute existing independently in the described, and it is a condition for the existence of knowledge, intent and the ability to perform actions out of choice. Life is also a necessary outcome of these - so every living thing has understanding, intention, and everything that has knowledge, intent and performs actions and performs actions out of choice is alive.

The noun 'modesty' is derived from 'life,' so the heart that is alive - it's owner is also alive - and it contains modesty which prevents it from performing evil and despicable actions, because in the modesty of the heart lies its immunity from these types of actions. This is why the Prophet (ﷺ) said; Modesty is from faith. And he said, Modesty and bashfulness are two branches from amongst the branches of faith, and obscenity and boasting are two branches from the branches of hypocrisy.

This is why the living being is clearly affected by despicable

28

actions, and he has an intent that prevents him from performing them in contravention to the One who is shameless because he is not alive and therefore has no modesty and therefore no faith that would restrain him from evil. So if the heart is alive and the person dies in its separation from the body, then the death of the soul lies in its separation from the body, not in the fact that it, in and of itself, has died - with the meaning of life leaving it. This is why Allah the Exalted said,

ولا تقولوا لمن يقتل في سبيل الله أموات بل أحياء   البقرة 154

. And say not of those who are killed in the Way of Allâh, "They are dead." Nay, they are living. Al-Baqara 2:154

ولا تحسبن الذين قتلوا في سبيل الله امواتا بل أحياء عند ربهم يرزقون   ال عمران 169

Think not of those who are killed in the Way of Allâh as dead. Nay, they are alive, Al-i-Imran 3:169

Despite the fact that they have died are included in His sayings,

كل نفس ذائقة الموت   ال عمران 185

Everyone shall taste death. Al-i-Imran 3:185

انك ميت وانهم ميتون   الزمر 30

Indeed you will die, and they will die. Az-Zumar 39:30

وهو الذي أحياكم ثم يميتكم ثم يحييكم عن الإنسان لكفور   سورة الحج 66

It is He, Who gave you life, and then will cause you to die, and will again give you life (on the Day of Resurrection). Verily man is indeed an ingrate. Al-Hajj 22:66

Therefore the death that is affirmed is not the same as the negated death. The affirmed death is the separation of the soul from the body, and the negated death is the leaving of life in totality from the body and soul. This is similar to the fact that sleep is the brother of death. Allah said,

الله يتوفى الأنفس حين موتها والتي لم تمت في منامها فيمسك التي قضى عليها الموت ويرسل الأخرى إلى أجل مسمى
الزمر 42

It is Allâh Who takes away the souls at the time of their death, and those that die not during their sleep. He keeps those (souls) for which He has ordained death and sends the rest for a term appointed. Az-Zumar 39:42

The Prophet (ﷺ) used to say when he awoke from sleep,

الحمد لله الذي أحيانا بعد ما أماتنا وإليه النشور

All praise is due to Allah Who gives us life after He had caused us to die and unto Him is the resurrection. In another hadith,

الحمد لله الذي عافاني في جسدي ورد علي روحي وأذن لي بذكره

All praise is due to Allah Who restored to my health and returned my soul and has allowed me to remember Him. When he lay down to sleep, he said,

اللهم إنك خلقت نفسي وانت توفاها لك مماتها ومحياها إن أحييتها فاحفظها وإن أمتها فاغفر لها اللهم إني اسألك العافية

O Allah, verily You have created my soul, and You shall take its life, to You belongs its death and life. If You should keep my soul alive then protect it, and if You should take its life then forgive it. O, Allah, I ask You to grant me good health. He said, With your name, O Allah, I die and live

ENVY IS A SICKNESS OF THE HEART

Some people said while explaining its meaning: 'Envy {hasad) is a grievance that befalls one due to the knowledge of the good condition of the wealthy. So in accordance with this, it is not possible that the person upon whom the blessings have been bestowed be jealous of these blessings because this person has them and is accustomed to them.

A group of people said: 'It is a desire to have the blessings removed from the one who is envied even if the one who is jealous does not attain the likes of these blessings. This is different from ghubta1 (also meaning envy) because it refers to a desire to possess the blessings bestowed upon the one who is envied but without the desire to see them removed from him.

The Types of Hasad

Strictly speaking, envy {hasad) is hatred and disliking the good condition of the envied one. This of two types:

1) Unrestricted dislike of the blessings bestowed upon the envied. This is the type of jealousy which incurs blame, so when one hates something he is then hurt and grieved by the existence of what he hates, and this becomes a sickness in his heart such that he takes pleasure in removal of the blessings from the envied even if this does not result in any benefit to him except for the single benefit of having the pain that was in his soul removed. But this pain is not removed except as a result of his continuously watching the envied so that the jealous person finds relief when the blessing is removed, but then it becomes more severe as is the case of the one who is sick, for it is possible that this blessing, or one similar to it, returns to the envied. This is why this second group said: 'It is a

desire to have the blessings removed,' for indeed the one who dislikes the blessings bestowed upon other than him desires to see them removed.

2) That he dislikes the superiority of that person over him, and he desires to be like him or better, so this is jealousy and has been called ghubta, and the Prophet (ﷺ) Called it hasad in the hadtth reported by both al-Bukharl and Muslim from the hadith of Ibn Mas'ud and Ibn 'Umar, {radiyAllahu 'anhum), that he (ﷺ) said: There is no envy (hasad) except in two cases: a person to whom Allah has granted wisdom, and he rules by this and teaches it to the people, and a person to whom Allah has granted wealth and property and along with this the power to spend it in the cause of Truth. This being the wording of Ibn Mas'ud. The wording of Ibn 'Umar, (Radi Allahu 'anhuma) is A person to whom Allah has given the Qur'an, and he recites it night and day, and a person to whom Allah has granted wealth and property from which he gives in charity night and day. Al-Bukhari also reports this hadith from Abu Hurayrah {radiyAlldhu (anhu), and its wording is, There is no desirable form of jealousy except for two types: a person to whom Allah has given the Qur'an and he recites it day and night, so when a person hears him he says, Tf only I were given the likes of what he has been given so that I may act upon it the way this person is..' And a person to whom Allah has bestowed wealth, and he spends in the cause of Truth, so a person says, Tf only I were given the likes of what he has been given, so that I may act upon it the way this person is.' So the Prophet (ﷺ) forbade hasad, with the exception of two cases which are referred to as al-ghubtay meaning that a person love the condition of someone else and dislike that this person be superior in this way (without his wishing that it be removed from that person). So if it is asked: 'Then why is this called envy when he loves only that Allah bestows these blessings upon him?' It is said, 'The starting point of this love is his looking towards the favors Allah has bestowed upon someone else and his disliking that this person be favored over him. So if this other person were not present, then he would not have desired these

blessings. So because the starting point of this love is this dislike that someone else be made superior to him, then this is called envy due to the love following the dislike. As for desiring that Allah bestows favors upon him without consideration of people's material conditions then this is not envy at all.'

This is why the generality of mankind have been tried with this second type of envy that has also been called al-munajasah (competition) because two people compete in a single desired matter, both of them trying to attain the same good. The reason for their trying to attain it is that one of them dislikes that the other be blessed with this matter over him just as any one of two competitors dislikes that other beat him. Competition is not considered blameworthy in general, rather it is considered to be praiseworthy when competing for righteousness, the Exalted said,

شْهَدُهُ الْمُقَرّبُونَ (٢١) إِنّ الْأَبْرَارَ لَفِي نَعِيمٍ (٢٢) عَلَى الْأَرَائِكِ يَنظُرُونَ (٢٣) تَعْرِفُ فِي وُجُوهِهِمْ نَضْرَةَ النّعِيمِ (٢٤) يُسْقَوْنَ مِن رّحِيقٍ مّخْتُومٍ (٢٥) خِتَامُهُ مِسْكٌ وَفِي ذَلِكَ فَلْيَتَنَافَسِ الْمُتَنَافِسُونَ (٢٦)

المطففين ٢١-٢٦

To which bear witness those nearest (to Allâh, i.e. the angels).22. Verily, Al-Abrâr (the pious believers of Islamic Monotheism) will be in Delight (Paradise).23. On thrones, looking (at all things).24. You will recognize in their faces the brightness of delight.25. They will be given to drink of pure sealed wine. So one is commanded to compete for these delights and not to compete for the delight of this fleeting world. Al-Mutaffifin 83:21-216

This is in total agreement to the hadith of the Prophet (ﷺ), for he forbade envy except of the one who has been granted knowledge and he acts according to it and teaches it, and the one who has been bestowed wealth and spends it (in the way of Allah). As for the one who has been granted knowledge but does not act upon this knowledge, or the one who has been bestowed wealth but does not spend this is obedience to Allah, then such a person is not to be envied and neither is his condition to be hoped for, for he is not in a state of good that is desirable, rather he is being presented with punishment. He also allowed jealousy for the one who has been given a responsibility, and he fulfils it with knowledge and justice and fulfills the trusts of its owners, and judges amongst the people by the Qur'an and Sunnah.

The station of such a person is lofty, but this only comes after a great amount of effort (Jihad) - the same is true of the mujahid. But the souls do not envy the one who is in severe hardship, and this is why the Prophet (ﷺ) did not mention it even though the mujahid, fighting in the Way of Allah, is superior to the one who is spending wealth. The opposite is true for the teacher and spender for they have no enemy in the physical world, but in the case that there were an enemy that they would have to per- form jihad against, then their ranking is more superior (than their station without having an enemy to fight). Similarly, the Prophet (ﷺ) did not mention the one who prays, fasts and performed the pilgrimage because there is no tangible benefit attained from the people for these actions by which the person can be exalted or disgraced, as can be attained in teaching and spending.

Between Hasad and Ghubta

Fundamentally, envy occurs when someone else attains power and authority; otherwise the one who is performing actions is not normally envied, even if this person be blessed with far more food, drink, and wives than others, as opposed to these two blessings of power and authority, for they cause a great deal of envy. This is why you find envy directed at the People of Knowledge, who have a following amongst the people that you will not find directed to others who do not have such a following. Similarly for the one who attracts a following due to his spending his wealth, for the people benefit this person by nourishing his heart, and this person brings benefit to them by nourishment of the bodies. Mankind is in need of that which will correct them in both these matters, this is why Allah, the one free from imperfection, has propounded two parables,

ضرب الله مثلا عبدا مملوكا لا يقدر على شيء ومن رزقناه منا رزقا حسنا فهو ينفق منه سرا وجهرا هل يستوون الحمد لله بل أكثرهم لا يعلمون * وضرب الله مثلا رجلين أحدهما أبكم لا يقدر على شيء وهو كل على مولاه أينما يوجهه لا يأت بخير هل يستوي هو ومن يأمر بالعدل وهو على صراط مستقيم   النحل 75 - 76

Allâh puts forward the example of (two men - a believer and a disbeliever); a slave (disbeliever) under the possession of another, he has no power of any sort, and (the other), a man (believer) on whom We have bestowed a good provision from Us, and he spends thereof secretly and openly. Can they be equal? (By no means). All the praises and thanks are to Allâh. Nay! (But) Most of them know not.7 5. And Allâh puts forward (another) example of two men, one of them dumb, who has no power over anything (disbeliever), and he is a burden on his master; whichever way he directs him, he brings no good. Is such a man equal to one (believer in the Islâmic Monotheism) who commands justice, and is himself on the Straight Path?. An-Nahl 16:75-76

These two parables were propounded by Allah for His Own Holy Self and for that which is worshipped besides Him, for indeed the idols are not capable of performing any actions that would be of benefit, and neither of saying anything that would be of benefit. So when a completely powerless slave under the possession of someone is considered, and another to whom Allah has provided a goodly provision from which he spends in secret and in the open, can this slave, incapable of doing good, and this person capable of doing good for the people in secret and open, ever be equal? And He, free is as He from defect, is able to bestow good upon His servants, and as He is continuously doing so. So how can this incapable slave (i.e., the idol) who cannot do anything, be likened to Allah to the extent that he is worshipped alongside Him? So this is the parable of one to whom Allah has bestowed wealth from which he spends day and night.

The second parable: when two people are considered, one of them is dumb, he does not understand not speak, and is not capable of anything and is, in fact, a burden upon his master, for whichever way he directs him he brings no good and hence he is of absolutely no use. The other is a just scholar - enjoining justice and acting justly, and is upon the Straight Path. This person is then like the one upon whom Allah has conferred wisdom, and he acts according to it and teaches it. And Allah has propounded this parable for Himself, for He is All-Knowing, All-Just, All-Powerful, commanding justice, He is maintaining His creation is justice is upon the Straight Way as He, the Exalted said,

$$\text{شهد الله أنه لا إله إلا هو والملائكة وأولو العلم قائما بالقسط لا إله إلا هو العزيز الحكيم}$$
$$\text{آل عمران 18}$$

Allâh bears witness that Lâ ilâha illa Huwa (none has the right to be worshipped but He), and the angels, and those having knowledge (also give this witness); (He always) maintains His creation in Justice. Lâ ilâha illa Huwa (none has the right to be worshipped but He), the All-Mighty, the All-Wise. Al-i-Imran 3:18

And He said upon the tongue of Hud,

$$\text{إن ربي على صراط مستقيم} \quad \text{هود 56}$$

Verily, my Lord is on the Straight Path (the truth). Hud 11:56

This is why the people used to exalt the home of al-'Abbas: 'Abdullah used to teach the people, and his brother used to feed them, and so they used to exalt them due to this.

Mu'awiyah, (radiyAllahu 'anhu), saw the people asking Ibn 'Umar about the rites of Hajj and Ibn 'Umar would give them the verdicts, to which Muawiyah said, 'By Allah, this is nobility' or something similar.

The Competition between as-Siddiq and 'Umar

So here is 'Umar bin al-Khattab {radiyAllahu 'anhu) competing with Abu Bakr {radiyAllahu 'anhu) with respect to spending in charity as is established in the Sahib (of al-Bukhari) from 'Umar bin al-Khattab, (radiyAllahu 'anhu), that he said:

The Messenger of Allah (ﷺ) commanded us to give in charity, and this coincided with my possessing some wealth. So I said (to myself): 'If there is a day that I can better Abu Bakr than it is this one.' So I went with half of my wealth, and the Messenger of Allah (ﷺ) asked me, 'What have you left for your family?' I replied, The same amount.' Then Abu Bakr came with everything that he possessed, and the Messenger of Allah (ﷺ) asked him, 'What have you left for your family?' He replied, 'I have left Allah and His Messenger for them.' So I said, 'I will never be able to better you in anything!'

type of jealousy (ghubta), but the state of as-Siddiq was better than his, and thus he would generally be the victor in such competition due to his indifference to the condition of others.

Moses Displays Ghubta

Likewise is the case with Prophet Musa as is mentioned in the hadith of Mr raj that he competed and felt jealousy towards the Prophet (ﷺ) to the point that he,

Cried due to the extent to which the Prophet (ﷺ) has surpassed him. So it was said to him, 'Why are you crying?' He replied, 'I am crying because there is a servant who shall be sent after me, and more of his nation shall enter Paradise than mine.

This hadith is also reported in other than the Sahib with a different wording,

We passed a person while he was saying in a loud voice, 'You have blessed him and honoured him (over me).' So we were raised to him and gave him our salam, he replied to our salam and said, 'Who is this with you O Jibra'il?' He said, 'This is Ahmad.' He said, 'Welcome O Illiterate Prophet who has conveyed the Message of his Lord and sincerely advised his nation.' Then we moved on, and I said, 'Who was this O Jibrail?' He replied, 'That was Musa bin 'Imran.' I said, 'And who was he censuring?' He replied, 'He was censuring your Lord with regards to you.' I said, 'He was raising his voice to His Lord?' He replied, 'Indeed Allah knew his truthfulness. 'So in this (Umar resembled Musa, and the condition of our Prophet (ﷺ) was superior to that of Musa for he did not possess any of this permissible jealousy.

Whoever Ranking Becomes Lofty; He is Secured from Ghubta

Similar to this from amongst the Sahabah were Abu 'Ubaydah bin Jarrah and those like him who were free from these types of concerns and due to this they were of a more exalted rank than those who would compete and display jealousy {ghubta) even though it was permitted. This is why Abu 'Ubaydah deserved to be called, The trusted one of this Unwtah!'

For if the one trusted does not have any rivalry and desire in his self for the things that he is entrusted with, then he is the most deserving of having the trust placed in him. The one who is known to possess no rivalry in greater matters is entrusted with the smaller matters, and the one is known to have no reason to steal from the wealth is entrusted with the wealth. As for the one who finds in himself treachery that resembles that of a wolf entrusted with sheep, then he is not able to discharge the trust placed in him due to his having in his heart a desire for what he is entrusted with.

It is reported in the Musnad of Ahmad from Anas, {radiyAllahua Anhu), that he said, We were sitting in the presence of the Messenger of Allah (ﷺ) one day and he said, 'A person is about to arrive from this mountain path who is from the people of Paradise.' So a person from the Ansar arrived, his beard dripping with the water of wudu and holding his sandals in his left hand, and he gave us the salam. The next day the Prophet (ﷺ) said words of similar import and the same person appeared in the same condition. On the third day the Prophet (ﷺ) again said words of similar import, and again this person appeared in the same condition, so when the Prophet (ﷺ) left, 'Abdullah bin 'Amr al-'As followed this person and said, 'indeed I have abused my father, and I swore that I would not go to him for three days so if you would let me stay with you until those three days expire* I would do so.' He replied, 'Yes.' Anas continued saying, So 'Abdullah told us that he spends three nights with this person yet he did not see him stand for the night prayer at all. All he did was when he turned sides on his bed he would mention Allah and make takbir and would do this until he stood for the Fajr prayer. 'Abdullah said, 'Except that I never heard him speak except good.' So when the three days were over, I was eager to make little of his actions. 1 said, 'Q servant of Allah there Was no hatred or disassociation between my father and me, but I heard the Messenger of Allah (ﷺ) saying on three occasions, 'A person is about to arrive who is from the people of Paradise,' and you arrived on those three occasions, so I wished to stay with you so that I may look at your actions and emulate them. But I have not seen you perform a great deal of actions, so what is it that has reached you to make the Messenger of Allah (ﷺ) say what he said?' He replied, 'It is nothing more than what you have seen, except that I do not find in myself any disloyalty to any of the Muslims, and neither do I find any jealousy for the wealth that Allah has bestowed upon them.' 'Abdullah said, 'This is that which has reached you and is something that we cannot endure.'

So in the saying of Abdullah bin 'Amr to him, 'This is something that has reached you and something that we cannot endure' lies an indication of his lack of jealousy and his being secure from all types of jealousy. This is why Allah praised the Ansar with His saying,

وَلَا يَجِدُونَ فِي صُدُورِهِمْ حَاجَةً مِمَّا أُوتُوا وَيُؤْثِرُونَ عَلَى أَنْفُسِهِمْ وَلَوْ كَانَ بِهِمْ خَصَاصَةٌ
الحشر 9

And have no jealousy in their breasts for that which they have been given (from the booty of Banû An-Nadîr), and give them (emigrants) preference over themselves even though they were in need of that. Al-Hashr 59:9

Meaning that which has been given to their brothers from the Muhajirun. The scholars of tafsir have stated: 'They do not find in their breasts jealousy and hatred for what has been given to the Muhajiruni Then some of them said, 'What has been given to them from the war booty.' And others said: 'What has been given to them of precedence and blessings' So they find no need of that which has been given the Muhdjirun of wealth and rank even though jealousy arises over these sorts of things.

Between the Aws and the Khazraj there existed competition in matters of religion, such that if one tribe were to do something for which they were regarded favourably by Allah and His Messenger, then the other tribe would desire to do the same. So this is competition in that which would bring them closer to Allah. Allah says,

ختامه مسك وفي ذلك فليتنافس المتنافسون   المطففين 26

He last thereof (that wine) will be the smell of Musk, and for this let (all) those strive who want to strive (i.e., hasten earnestly to the obedience   of   Allah).   Al-Mutaffifin   83:2

BLAMEWORTHY JEALOUSY

As for the jealousy that is totally blameworthy then Allah has said with regards to the people of the Scripture,

ود كثير من أهل الكتاب لو يردونكم من بعد إيمانكم كفارا حسدا من عند أنفسهم من بعد
ما تبين لهم الحق   البقرة 109

Many of the people of the Scripture (Jews and Christians) wish that if they could turn you away as disbelievers after you have believed, out of envy from their ownselves, even after the truth

(that Muhammad (ﷺ) is Allâh's Messenger) has become manifest unto them. Al-Baqara 2:109

'They wish' meaning that they hope to make you apostasies from your religion out of jealousy. So jealousy was the deciding factor behind their wish even after the Truth has been made clear to them. This is because when they saw you attain what you attained of blessings - in fact, they saw you attain that which they themselves had never attained - they became jealous of you. Similarly this is mentioned in another verse,

أَمْ يَحْسُدُونَ النَّاسَ عَلَىٰ مَا آتَاهُمُ اللَّهُ مِن فَضْلِهِ فَقَدْ آتَيْنَا آلَ إِبْرَاهِيمَ الْكِتَابَ وَالْحِكْمَةَ
وَآتَيْنَاهُم مُّلْكًا عَظِيمًا (54) فَمِنْهُم مَّنْ آمَنَ بِهِ وَمِنْهُم مَّن صَدَّ عَنْهُ وَكَفَىٰ بِجَهَنَّمَ سَعِيرًا
النساء 54 – 55

Or do they envy men (Muhammad (ﷺ) and his followers) for what Allâh has given them of His Bounty? Then We had already given the family of Ibrâhîm (Abraham) the Book and Al-Hikmah (As-Sunnah - Divine Revelation to those Prophets not written in the form of a book) and conferred upon them a great kingdom.54. Of them were (some) who believed in him (Muhammad صلى الله

41

عليه وسلم), and of them were (some) who averted their faces from
him (Muhammad ﷺ); and enough is Hell for burning (them).
An-Nisa 4:54-55

قُلْ أَعُوذُ بِرَبِّ النَّاسِ. مَلِكِ النَّاسِ. إِلَهِ النَّاسِ. مِن شَرِّ الْوَسْوَاسِ الْخَنَّاسِ. الَّذِي يُوَسْوِسُ
فِي صُدُورِ النَّاسِ. مِنَ الْجِنَّةِ وَالنَّاسِ.   الناس 1 - 5

Say: "I seek refuge with (Allâh) the Lord of mankind,1. "The King
of mankind, 2."The Ilâh (God) of mankind, 3. "From the evil of the
whisperer (devil who whispers evil in the hearts of men) who
withdraws (from his whispering in one's heart after one remembers
Allâh).4. "Who whispers in the breasts of mankind. 5."Of jinn and
men." 6. An-Nas 114:1-6

A group of scholars of Tafsir mentioned that this Surah was
revealed due to the jealousy of the Jews harboured towards the
Messenger of Allah (ﷺ)to the extent that they performed magic
on him. The magic was done by the Jew, Labld bin al-'Asam.' So
the one who is jealous, hating the favours bestowed by Allah upon
someone else is an oppressor, going beyond bounds due to this. As
for the one who dislikes that someone else be blessed and wishes
to be blessed in the same way, then this is forbidden for him except
in that which will bring him closer to Allah. So if he were to wish
for something that has been given to someone else which would
help bring him closer to Allah, then there is no problem in this.
However, his wishing for it in his heart, without looking to the
condition of someone else is better and more excellent.

Then if this person were to act, dictated by this jealousy, he would
be an oppressor going beyond bounds, deserving of punishment
unless he repents. So the one who is affected by the one who is
jealous is oppressed and should be enjoined to patience and taqwa.
He should be patient of the harm afflicted upon him by the one
who is jealous, and he should forgive and overlook, just as Allah
said,

ود كثير من أهل الكتاب لو يردونكم من بعد إيمانكم كفارا حسدا من عند أنفسهم من بعد
ما تبين لهم الحق   البقرة 109

Many of the people of the Scripture (Jews and Christians) wish that if they could turn you away as disbelievers after you have believed, out of envy from their ownselves, even after the truth (that Muhammad (ﷺ) is Allâh's Messenger) has become manifest unto them. Al-Baqara 2:109

Indeed Yusuf, ('alayhis salam) was tried by the jealousy of his brothers:

إِذْ قَالُوا لَيُوسُفُ وَأَخُوهُ أَحَبُّ إِلَى أَبِينَا مِنَّا وَنَحْنُ عُصْبَةٌ إِنَّ أَبَانَا لَفِي ضَلَالٍ مُبِينٍ
يوسف 8

When they said: "Truly, Yûsuf (Joseph) and his brother (Benjamin) are dearer to our father than we, while we are a strong group. Really, our father is in a plain error. Yusuf 12:8

So they were envied due to their father favouring them over the rest of the brothers, which is why Yaqub said to Yusuf,

قال يا بني لا تقصص رؤياك على إخوتك فيكيدوا لك كيدا إن الشيطان للإنسان عدو مبين يوسف 5

He (the father) said: "O my son! Relate not your vision to your brothers, lest they should arrange a plot against you. Verily! Shaitân (Satan) is to man an open enemy!. Yusuf 12:5

They went on to oppress him by discussing his murder and throwing him in the well, and his being sold as a slave by the ones who took him to the land of the disbelievers, and his subsequently being owned by these disbelieving people. Then after being oppressed, Yusuf was tried by the one who invited him to an indecent deed and attempted to seduce him, and she sought aid from anyone who would help her in this, but he was preserved from this. Instead, he chose to be imprisoned rather than perform this indecent deed, preferring the punishment of this world rather than the Displeasure of Allah (in the Hereafter).

Hence he was oppressed by the one who desired him due to her base desires and her corrupt objective. So this love with which she desired him arose as a result of her succumbing to the vain desires of her heart, and its happiness or sadness lay in his accepting or rejecting the temptation. He was also oppressed by those who hated him with a hatred that led to his being thrown in the well, then his becoming captive and owned without his choice. Therefore these people removed him from the absolute freedom that he enjoyed to becoming forced into slavery to the false worshippers. This forced him to seek refuge in the prison out of his own free will, thereby making his trial greater.

His patience on this occasion arose out of his own volition coupled with his fear of Allah, thus differing from his patience at their oppression, which was having patience at the onset of calamities, and if one were not to be patient at the likes of these then he would take to the way of mere animals.

This second type of patience, arising from one's free will, is the more excellent of the two. This is why Allah said,

إنه من يتق ويصبر فإن الله لا يضيع أجر المحسنين   يوسف 90

Verily, he who fears Allâh with obedience to Him (by abstaining from sins and evil deeds, and by performing righteous good deeds), and is patient, then surely, Allâh makes not the reward of the Muhsinûn (good-doers) to be lost. Yusuf 12:90

Likewise when the believer is harmed due to his faith; and disbelief, transgression, and disobedience is sought from him - and if he were not to accept this then he would be harmed and punished - then he should choose this harm and punishment over renegading from his religion - even if it results in imprisonment or banishment from his land - just as was done by the Muhajirun in their choosing to leave their settlements rather than leave their religion for which they were harmed and punished.

The Prophet (ﷺ) was harmed in a number of different ways, but he was patient through-out this with a patience that arose out of his own volition, and indeed he was harmed in this way only that he may do what he did out of his own choice. So this patience of his was greater than the patience of Yusuf, for only an indecent action was sought from Yusuf, and he was only punished by imprisonment when he did not comply. But disbelief was sought from the Prophet (;|g) and his Companions, and when they did not do this - then they were punished by being slaughtered, and other such harms - the least of which was imprisonment, for the polytheists imprisoned him and Ban! Has him for a time in a mountain pass. Then when Abu Talib died, they became more severe against him, and when the Ansar gave him the pledge of the allegiance and when the polytheists came to know of this they tried to prevent him from leaving (for .Yladlnah) and tried to detain him and his Companions. Then all of them emigrated secretly except for 'Umar bin al-Khattab and those like him.

So what befell the believers came about as a result of their choosing obedience to Allah and His Messenger, and it was not from the afflictions that occur without the servant's choice of the type that Yusuf was tried with, and neither of the type of his being separated from his father. So this patience endured by the believers was the nobler of the two types of patience, and its possessors are greater with respect to ranking. This, even though the one who is tried without his will shall be rewarded for his patience and his contentment with the decree of Allah, and his sins will be expiated. As for the person who is tried and harmed for choosing obedience to Allah, then he will be rewarded for the actual trial, and it shall be written as a righteous action for him, Allah, the Most High, said,

ذلك بأنهم لا يصيبهم ظمأ ولا نصب ولا مخمصة في سبيل الله ولا يطئون موطئا يغيظ الكفار ولا ينالون من عدو نيلا إلا كتب لهم به عمل صالح إن الله لا يضيع أجر المحسنين   التوبة 120

That is because they suffer neither thirst nor fatigue, nor hunger in the Cause of Allâh, nor they take any step to raise the anger of disbelievers nor inflict any injury upon an enemy but is written to their credit as a deed of righteousness. Surely, Allâh wastes not the reward of the Muhsinûn. At-Tawba 9:120

This contrasting with the case of the one who is tried without his choice, such as being sick, or death, or a thief stealing from him - this person shall be rewarded for his patience only, not for the actual trial itself and what results from it. As for those who are harmed due to their faith in Allah and obedience to Him and His Messenger, and as a result of this they are in pain, or are sick, or are imprisoned, or are forced to leave their land, or their property and family is taken from them, or are beaten and abused, or their position and wealth is diminished, then in this they are upon the way of the Prophets and those that followed them such as the Muhdjirun.

So these people shall be rewarded for what has harmed them, and a righteous action shall be written for them due to it just as the mujahid shall be rewarded for the hunger, thirst and fatigue that afflicts him, and for enraging the disbelievers even if these effects are not something he has physically set out to do, but they are resultant from his action (of performing jihad) that he has chosen to do. The people have differed over this: can it be said that these resultant effects are actions of the actor of the reason for these effects, or are they Actions of Allah, or is there no actor for them? What is correct is that they are shared between the actor of the reason and the (Actor of the) totality of the reasons, and this is why a righteous action is written for him.

The purpose behind this discussion is that jealousy is one of the sicknesses of the soul, and it is an illness that afflicts the generality of mankind, and only a few are secure from it. This is why it is said: The body is never free from jealousy, but debasement brings it out, and nobility hides it. It was said to al-Hasan al-Basrl, 'Can a believer be envied?' He replied, 'What has made you forget Yusuf and his brothers, have you no father?' But you should keep (this envy should it occur) blinded in your heart, for you cannot be harmed by that which you did not act upon in speech or action.'

The Cure for Jealousy

So the one who finds that he harbors jealousy in his soul towards someone else, then it is upon him to treat it with patience and taqwa of Allah, and dislike it being in his soul. Many religious people do not take a stance against the one who is envied and neither do they help the one who would oppress him, but neither do they establish what is obligatory with respect to his rights. Rather when someone censures the one who is envied they do not agree with or aid him in the censure but neither do they mention his praiseworthy qualities. Likewise, if someone were to praise him, they remain silent. So these people are responsible for their leaving what is commanded with respect to the rights of the envied, and they have exceeded the proper bounds in this even though they may not have taken a stance against him. The reward of these people is that their rights, in turn, will be neglected and on some occasions, they will not be treated fairly, and neither will they be helped against the one who oppresses them, just as they did not aid the envied who was oppressed. As for the one who actually takes a stance against the envied, either with words or actions then he will be punished for this, and the one who fears Allah and is patient and does not become one of the oppressors - Allah will benefit him for his taqwa.

The Causes for Jealousy

This is what occurred with Zaynab bint Jahsh (radiyAllahu (anha) for she used to be one who would vie with 'A'ishah from the wives of the Prophet (ﷺ) The jealousy displayed by some women to others is great, and is especially true of those who are married to one husband. The woman will go to great extents to get her allotted time from him for sometimes some of her allotted time will be missed due to his sharing with other wives. This jealousy commonly occurs amongst those that share authority or property in the case when some of them take a share from it, and others are left with none. It also occurs between those that debate, due to their hatred that their opponent gets the better of them, such as the jealousy of the brothers of Yusuf, or the jealousy of the two sons of Adam one to the other for in this case the brother was envied by the other due to Allah accepting his sacrifice and not the other's, this leading to his murder. Also, the jealousy displayed towards the Muslims by the Jews. It was said,

The first sins by which Allah was disobeyed were three: covetousness, arrogance, and jealousy. Covetousness was displayed by Adam, arrogance by Iblis, and jealousy from Qabil when he killed Habil.

In the *hadith* there occurs: There are three sins from which no one can be saved: jealousy, suspicion, and omens. Shall I tell you of what would remove you from this: when you envy then do not hate, when you are suspicious then do not actualize your suspicions, and when you see omens then ignore them. "
Reported by Ibn Abi ad-Dunya from the *hadith* of Abu Hurayrah, *radiyAllahu (anhu)*.

In the *Sunan* from the Prophet (ﷺ),

You have been afflicted with the illness of the nations that came before you - jealousy and hatred. They are the shearers; I do not mean shearers of the hair, rather they are shearers of the religion.

So he called jealousy an illness just as he called miserliness an illness in his saying, And what illness is worse than miserliness. And in another hadith, I seek refuge with You from the evil morals and manners, vain desires and illnesses.

Mentioning illnesses alongside manners and vain desires. Manners are those things that the soul becomes accustomed to such that they become its nature and disposition. Allah said in this regard,

وانك لعلى خلق عظيم   القلم 4

And Verily, you (O Muhammad (ﷺ)) are on an exalted (standard of) character. Al-Qalam 68:4

Ibn 'Abbas, Ibn 'Uyaynah and Ahmad ibn Hanbal {radiyAllahu (an hum) said in commentary to this:

Meaning 'upon a great religion.'

And in a variant wording of Ibn 'Abbas:

The religion of Islam.'

This was similarly stated by 'A'ishah {radiyAlldhu (anha)

His manners were the Qur'an,

and Hasan al-Basri,

The manners of the Qur'an is 'the exalted standard of character.'

The manners of the Qur'an is 'the exalted standard of character.'

As for 'vain desires' then they are temporary anomalous conditions, and 'illness' is sickness - this is an affliction that harms the heart and corrupts it. In the first hadith jealousy was mentioned along with hatred. This is because the envier, first of all, dislikes the bounty bestowed by Allah upon the one who is envied, and then begins hating this person. This is because the hatred of the thing being bestowed leads to hatred of the one upon whom it is bestowed, for when the blessings of Allah are bestowed upon an individual, he would love that they go away, and they would not go away except by the one who is envied going away. Therefore he hates him and loves that he not be there. Jealousy necessarily leads to desire and hatred just as Allah informed us of those that came before us: that they differed,

آل عمران 19   بعد ما جاءهم العلم بغيا بينهم

Out of mutual jealousy, after knowledge had come to them. Al-i-Imran 3:19

So their differing did not arise due to the lack of knowledge, rather they knew the Truth, but it was due to some of them hating others, just as the envier hates the envied.

In Sahibs of al-Bukhari and Muslim, Anas bin Malik (radiyAllahu (anhu) reports that the Prophet (ﷺ) said,

Do not envy each other, do not hate each other, do not oppose each other, and do not cut relations, rather be servants of Allah as brothers. It is not permissible for a Muslim to disassociate from his brother for more than three days such that they meet and one ignores the other, and the best of them is the one 'who initiates the salam.

He (ﷺ) said, in the hadith that is agreed to be authentic, reported by Anas also,

By the One in Whose Hand is my soul, none of you believes until he loves for his brother what he loves for himself.

Allah, the Most High, said,

وَإِنَّ مِنْكُمْ لَمَنْ لَيُبَطِّئَنَّ فَإِنْ أَصَابَتْكُمْ مُصِيبَةٌ قَالَ قَدْ أَنْعَمَ اللّهُ عَلَيَّ إِذْ لَمْ أَكُنْ مَعَهُمْ شَهِيداً (72) وَلَئِنْ أَصَابَكُمْ فَضْلٌ مِنَ اللّهِ لَيَقُولَنَّ كَأَنْ لَمْ تَكُنْ بَيْنَكُمْ وَبَيْنَهُ مَوَدَّةٌ يَا لَيْتَنِي كُنْتُ مَعَهُمْ فَأَفُوزَ فَوْزاً عَظِيماً   النساء 72 – 73

There is certainly among you he who would linger behind (from fighting in Allah's Cause). If a misfortune befalls you, he says, "Indeed Allah has favored me in that I was not present among them."72. But if a bounty (victory and booty) comes to you from Allah, he would surely say - as if there had never been ties of affection between you and him - "Oh! I wish I had been with them; then I would have achieved a great success (a good share of booty)." An-Nisa 4:73-72

So these people who lingered behind did not love for their Muslim brothers what they loved for themselves, rather if the Muslims were afflicted with a calamity, they were overjoyed that it only afflicted them, and if they met with blessings they were not happy for them, rather they wished that they too had a portion of this blessing. So they would not become happy except if they received something of this world or some evil of this world was diverted from them. This was due to them not loving Allah and His Messenger and the Home of the Hereafter, for if this had been the case, they would have loved their brothers, and loved what they had received of His blessings and they would have been hurt by the calamity that had afflicted them.

As for the one who is not made happy by what has made the Muslims happy, and is not grieved by what has made the Muslims grieve then he is not of them. In the Sahibs of al-Bukhari and Muslim from 'Amir ash-Sha'bI who said: "I heard an-Nu'man bin Bashir delivering a sermon and saying: I heard the Messenger of Allah (ﷺ) saying,

The similitude of the believers with respect to, their mutual love, mutual mercy, and mutual kindness in like that of one body. When a part of it suffers, the whole body suffers with fever and sleeplessness.16

In the Sahibs of al-Bukhari and Muslim from the hadith of Abu Musa. al-Ashfari, radiyAllahu (anhu), who said: "The Messenger of Allah (ﷺ) said,

The Muslim to another Muslim is like a building, one part of it strengthens another, and he interlaced his fingers.

Between Jealousy and Miserliness

Greed is a sickness as is miserliness, and jealousy is worse than miserliness as occurs in the hadith reported by Abu Dawud from the Prophet (ﷺ) that he said,

Jealousy eats away good deeds, just as fire eats away firewood, and giving charity extinguishes sins just as water extinguishes the fire.

This is because the miser only stops himself from having good, but the envier dislikes the favors of Allah bestowed upon His servants. It is possible that a person give to those lesser than him who would help him achieve his objectives and yet display jealousy to those of the same level as him just as it is possible for him to be miserly without displaying envy to others. Greed is the basis for this as Allah said,

الحشر 9   ومن يوق شح نفسه فأولئك هم المفلحون

And whosoever is saved from his own covetousness, such are they who will be the successful. Al-Hashr 59:9

In the Sahibs of al-Bukhari and Muslim the Prophet (ﷺ) said,

Beware of greed for it destroyed those that came before you: it commanded them to be miserly and they were, it commanded them to be oppressive and they were and it commanded them to break the ties of kinship and they did.20

(Abdur-Rahman bin ' Awf used to frequently say in his supplication while make Tawaf,

'O Allah! Save my soul from greed.' So a person said to him, 'Why is this your most frequent supplication?' He replied, 'When I safeguard myself from greed, I safeguard myself from greed, miserliness and from severing the ties of kinship.' And jealousy necessarily leads to oppression.

THE DISEASE OF DESIRES AND PASSIONATE LOVE

Between Jealousy and Desires

Miserliness and jealousy are sicknesses that lead to the soul hating that which would benefit it, and its loving that which would harm it. This is why jealousy was mentioned alongside hatred and resentment in the preceding hadiths. As for the sickness of desire and passionate love then this is the soul loving that which would harm it and coupled with this is its hatred of that which would benefit it.

Passionate love is a psychological sickness, and when its effects become noticeable on the body, it becomes a sickness that afflicts the mind also. Either by afflicting the mind by the likes of melancholy, or afflicting the body through weakness and emaciation. But the purpose here is to discuss its effect on the heart, for passionate love is the fundament that makes the soul covet that which would harm it, similar is the one weak of body who covets that which harms it, and if he is not satiated by that then he is grieved, and if he is satiated then his sickness increases.

The Reality of Passionate love (ishq)

The same applies to the heart afflicted with this love, for it is harmed by its connection to the loved, either by seeing, touching, hearing, even think about it. And if he were to curb the love then the heart is hurt and grieved by this, and if he gives in to the desire, then the sickness becomes stronger and becomes a means through which the grievance is increased.

In the hadith there occurs,

Indeed Allah shelters His believing servant from the world just as one of you shelter your sick ones from food and drink (that would harm them).

In the hadith concerning the saving of Musa reported by Wahb, which is recorded by Imam Ahmad in az-Zuhd,

Allah says: 'Indeed I drive away My friends from the delights of this world and its opulence and comfort just as the compassionate shepherd drives away his camel from the dangerous grazing lands. And indeed I make them avoid its tranquility and livelihood, just as the compassionate shepherd makes his camel to avoid the resting-places wherein it would be easy prey. This is not because I consider them to be insignificant, but so that they may complete their portion of My Kindness in safety and abundance, the delights of the world will not attract him and neither would desires overcome him.'

Therefore the only cure for the sick lies in his removing the sickness by removing this blameworthy love from his heart.

People are divided into two opinions concerning passionate love: One group says that if falls into the category of intentions and wishes, this being the famous opinion. Another groups says that it falls into the category of imagination and fantasies and that it is a corruption of the imagination since it causes one to depict the one who is loved in other than his true reality. This group went on to say:

And this is why Allah has not been described with passionate love (ishk) and neither that He passionately loves (ya'shik) because He is far removed from this, and one cannot be praised who has these corrupt thoughts.
As for the first group, then from them are those who said:
'He is described with passionate love (ishk) because it is a complete and perfect love and Allah loves (yuhib)
And it is reported in the narration of 'Abdul Wahid bin Zayd that He said,
'The servant will always continue to draw closer to me, loving Me and I loving him (A'shiquhu)?
This is the saying of some of the Sufis but the majority do not

apply this word to Allah, because passionate love is a love exceeding the proper bounds, as for the Love of Allah then it has no end and cannot exceed the proper bounds. Passionate love is to be considered blameworthy without any exceptions, it is not to be praised when it is directed towards the Creator or created because it is a love that exceeds the proper bounds.

This is also true because the word 'passionate love' is only employed with regards to a man loving a woman or child (or vice versa), it is not employed in things such as the love of one's family, property or status, just as it is not employed with regards to the love of the Prophets and the righteous. Commonly, you will find this word being mentioned alongside a forbidden action, such as loving the woman who is not lawful for him, or loving a child joined with the unlawful glance and touch and other such unlawful actions.

As for the love of a man for his wife or slave-girl which leads him out of the folds of justice such that he does unlawful things for her and leaves what is obligatory - as commonly happens - even to the extent that he may oppress his son born of his old wife due to this love of his new wife, or to the extent that he will do things to keep her happy that would harm his religion and worldly life. For example his singling her out for inheritance that she does not deserve, or that he gives her family authority and property that exceeds the limits set by Allah, or he goes to excesses in spending on her, or he makes unlawful things possible for her which harms his religion and worldly life. This passionate love is forbidden with regards to one who is permissible for him, so how would it be with regards for one who has passionate love for someone who is unlawful Or with regards to two men? For this contains a corruption the extent of which none can assess except the Lord of the servants; it is a sickness that corrupts the religion and objectives of the one who possesses it, then it corrupts his intelligence and then his body. Allah, the Most High, says,

يَا نِسَاءَ النّبِيّ لَسْتُنَّ كَأَحَدٍ مِنَ النّسَاءِ إِن اتّقَيْتُنّ فلا تَخْضَعْنَ بِالْقَوْل فَيَطْمَعَ الّذِي فِي قَلْبِهِ مَرَضٌ وَقُلْنَ قَوْلاً مَعْرُوفا سورة الأحزاب 32

O wives of the Prophet! You are not like any other women. If you keep your duty (to Allâh), then be not soft in speech, lest he in whose heart is a disease (of hypocrisy, or evil desire for adultery) should be moved with desire, but speak in an honorable manner. Al-Ahzab 33:32

There are some whose hearts contain the disease of desire and whose perceptions are only skin deep. When the object of the desire submits, the sickness is satiated, and this satiation strengthens the desire and pursuit of the object and hence strengthens the sickness. This is in contrast to the one whose objective is not meg for this failure results in removing the satiation that would strengthen the sickness and thereby the desire is weakened as is the love. This is because the person definitely intends that there be action accompanying his desire, for Otherwise all his desire would be is just whisperings of the soul, unless there is some speech or looking accompanying this.

As for the one who is afflicted with this passionate love but holds back and is patient, then indeed Allah will reward him for his Taqwa as occurs in the hadith.

That the one who passionately loves someone yet holds hack, conceals this and is patient, then dies upon this, will be a martyr.

But it is known from the evidences of the Shari'ah that if one were to hold hack from performing that which is unlawful, be it looking, speaking or acting, and he conceals this and does not articulate it so as not to fall into that which is prohibited and he is patient in his obedience to Allah and keeping away from disobedience to Allah, despite the pain that his heart feels due to passionate love, (similar to the case of the one who is patient through a calamity), then indeed this person would gain the same reward as those who have feared Allah and been patient.

انه من يتق ويصبر فان الله لا يضيع أجر المحسنين سورة يوسف 90

Verily, he who fears Allâh with obedience to Him (by abstaining from sins and evil deeds, and by performing righteous good deeds), and is patient, then surely, Allâh makes not the reward of the Muhsinûn (good-doers) to be lost. Yusuf 12:90

This holds true for the disease of envy and all other sicknesses that afflict the heart. So when the soul pursues that which would anger Allah, and the person prevents himself from this, fearing Allah, then he is included in His saying,

سورة   وأما من خاف مقام ربه ونهى النفس عن الهوى * فإن الجنة هي المأوى
النازعات 40-41

But as for him who feared standing before his Lord, and restrained himself from impure evil desires and lusts.40. Verily, Paradise will be his abode. An-Nazi'at 79:40-41

When the soul loves Something, it will do all that it can to attain it, so the One who does this out of having a blameworthy love or hatred then this action of his would be sinful. For example his hating a person due to envying him and thereby harming whosoever is linked to that person - either by preventing his rights or by showing them enmity, or his doing something that is commanded by Allah but he does it due to his desires and not for the sake of Allah.

These types of sicknesses are commonly found in the heart. The person can hate something and due to this hate, love a great many things due to mere whims and fancies. As one poet affected by this said,

'Tor the sake of a Sudanese girl he loved Sudan to the point that he loved the black dogs due to his love of her.'

So he loved a black girl, and therefore loved all types of black even the blackness of dogs! All of this is a sickness in the heart with regards to its imagination, fantasies and desires. We ask Allah that He eliminate all of the illnesses from our hearts, and we seek refuge with Allah from evil manners, desires and sicknesses.

The Natural Inclination of the Heart is to love of Allah]

The heart has only been created for the worship of Allah, and this is the natural disposition fitrah) upon which Allah created His servants as the Prophet (□) said,

Every new-born child is born upon the natural disposition and it is his parents that make him a Jew, Christian or a Magian, as an animal produces a perfect young animal, do you see any part of its body amputated?

Then Abu Hurayrah, (radiyAllahu (anhu), said, recite if you wish the saying of Allah,

فطرت الله التي فطر الناس عليها
سورة الروم 30

Allâh's Fitrah (i.e. Allâh's Islâmic Monotheism) with which He has created mankind. Ar-Rum 30:30

So Allah has made the natural disposition of His servants to love Him and worship Him Alone, so if the natural disposition was to be left as it is without corrupting it, then it Would be cognizant of Allah, loving Him Alone; but the natural disposition does become corrupted due to the sickness of the heart - such as the parents making it a Jew or a Christian - even though this be by the Will and Predecree of Allah, just like the body is altered by amputation. But even after this it is possible for the heart to return to the natural disposition if Allah makes this easy for the one who does his utmost to return it to the natural disposition.

The Messengers were sent to affirm and re-establish the natural disposition and to perfect it, not to alter it. So when the heart loves Allah Alone, making the religion sincerely for Him, it will not be tried by the love of anyone else, not to mention be tried with passionate love because were it to be afflicted with passionate love then this would diminish its loving Allah alone. This is why when Yusuf was tried with this passionate love (directed to him) his love of Allah Alone, making the religion sincerely for him, did not allow him to be overcome by this, rather Allah said,

لولا أن رأى برهان ربه كذلك لنصرف عنه السوء والفحشاء إنه من عبادنا
المخلصين   سورة يوسف 24

had he not seen the evidence of his Lord. Thus it was, that We might turn away from him evil and illegal sexual intercourse. Surely, he was one of Our chosen (guided) slaves. Yusuf 12:24

As for the wife of al-ʿAziz, it was because she was and her nation were polytheists that she was afflicted with passionate love. No one, is afflicted with passionate love except that this diminishes his singling out Allah Alone for worship and his faith. The heart that repents to Allah, fearing Him, has two routes by which it can remove this passionate love:

Preventative Measures from Passionate Love

1) Repenting to Allah and loving Him, for indeed this is more satisfying and purer than anything else, and nothing will be left to love alongside Allah.

2) Fearing Allah, for indeed fear is the opposite of passionate love and removes it So everyone who loves something, with passion or otherwise, then this love can be removed by loving that which is more beloved to compete with it.

This love can also be removed by fearing the occurrence of a harm that is more hateful to one than leaving this love. So when Allah is more beloved to the servant than anything else, and more feared by him than anything else, then he will not fall into passionate love or find any love that would compete with his love of Allah, except in the case of negligence or at a time when this love and fear has become weak by his leaving some of the obligatory duties and by performing some of the prohibited actions. For indeed faith increases with obedience and decreases with disobedience, so each time a servant obeys Allah out of love and fear, and leaves a prohibited action out of love and fear, his love and fear becomes stronger, and any love or fear of anything else besides Allah will disappear from his heart.

Some Cures for the Heart

The same is true for the sickness of the body: for the health of the body is preserved by the same, and the sickness is repressed by the opposite. The correctness of the faith in the heart is preserved by its like, meaning that which would breed faith in the heart from the beneficial knowledge and righteous action for these are its nourishment as occurs in the hadith of Ibn Mas'ud, reported as his saying and as a hadith of the Messenger (□)

Indeed every host loves that people come to his table spread, and indeed the table spread of Allah is the Qur'an.

So the Qur'an is the table spread of Allah.

From those things that nourish the heart are supplication at the end of the night, the times of Adhan and Iqamah, in his prostration, at the ends of the prayers6 - add to this repentance. For indeed the one who repents to Allah and then in turn Allah forgives him, He will then give him enjoyment for an appointed time. That he takes to reciting the reported adhkdr for the day and at the time he sleeps. That he bears with patience what he is enticed with that would divert him from all of this, for Allah will immediately aid him with a spirit from Him and write faith in his heart. That he be eager to complete the obligatory duties such as the five prayers inwardly and outwardly for they are the pillars of the religion. That his words of recourse be

""لا حول ولا قوة إلا بالله
la hawla wa la quwwata illa billah

for by them heavy burdens can be born, horrors can be overcome, and the servant be gifted with the best of conditions to live in. That he should not give up the supplication and seeking help from Allah, for the servant will be answered as long as he is not hasty, saying

1 have supplicated and supplicated but 1 have not been answered.

That he should know that help comes with patience, that relief comes after anxiety and distress, that after every period of difficulty there follows a period a period of ease.

That he knows that no prophet or one less than him was rewarded with a good end except as a result of his being patient.

And all praise and thanks are due to Allah, the Lord of Creation. To Him belongs praise and grace for guiding us to Islam and the Sunnah, a praise that Would suffice His favours to us outwardly and inwardly, as in required for the nobility of His Face and might of His Magnificence. Abundant Peace and Blessings be upon our master, Muhammad (^), and upon his family, Companions, his wives - the mothers of the believers, and all those that follow them in   good   until   the   Day   of   Judge

Ibn Taymiyyah

author bio

Taqī ad-Dīn Ahmad ibn Taymiyyah (Arabic: تقي الدين أحمد ابن تيمية January 22, 1263 - September 26, 1328), known as Ibn Taymiyyah for short, Sunni Muslim theologian, jurisconsult, logician, and reformer.

www.ingramcontent.com/pod-product-compliance
Lightning Source LLC
Chambersburg PA
CBHW071634040426
42452CB00009B/1618